Spies and Spying

SECRET SERVICES

Anne Rooney

Smart Apple Media

Smart Apple Media
P.O. Box 3263
Mankato, MN 56002

Printed in the United States of America

Library of Congress Cataloging-in-Publication Data

Rooney, Anne.
  Secret services / Anne Rooney.
     p. cm. -- (Spies and spying)
  Includes index.
  ISBN 978-1-59920-360-7 (hardcover)
  1. Intelligence service--United States--Juvenile literature. I. Title.
  JK468.I6 S3962010
  363.28'3--dc22
                           2008055504

Created by Q2AMedia
Editor: Honor Head
Art Director: Rahul Dhiman
Designer: Ranjan Singh
Picture Researcher: Shreya Sharma
Line Artist: Sibi N. Devasia
Coloring Artist: Mahender Kumar

All words in **bold** can be found in the glossary on pages 30–31.

Web site information is correct at time of going to press. However, the publishers cannot
accept liability for any information or links found on third-party web sites.

Picture credits
t=top b=bottom c=center l=left r=right
Cover Images: Mary/ Shutterstock, Inset: Army.Mil: t, Q2AMedia: c, Q2AMedia: b.

Insides: Steven Vidler/ Eurasia Press/ Corbis: 4, Jormala/ Fotolia: 5, U.S. Department of Energy, National Nuclear Security
Administration, Nevada Site Office: 8, Bettmann/ Corbis: 9tr, Bertie Coetzee/ Shutterstock: 10t, spectral/ 123RF: 11b, Frank Naylor /
Alamy: 12, Associated Press: 13tr, Régis Bossu/ Sygma/ Corbis: 14, keella/ Shutterstock: 15bl, Antoine Gyori/ Corbis Sygma: 16, Doug
Mills/ Associated Press: 17, Jeffrey L. Rotman/ Corbis: 18, Steinmetz/ Corbis: 19, Anthony Potter/ Corbis: 20, Sgt. S. D. Brown/ U.S
Department of Defense: 21, Jim McDonald/ Corbis: 22, Bettmann/ Corbis: 23, Bettmann/ Corbis: 24, Wildbirdimages/ Dreamstime: 26,
Rex Features: 27, Associated Press: 28, Feng Li/ Staff / Getty Images AsiaPac/ Getty Images: 29.

Q2AMedia Art Bank: 6, 7, 9bl, 10b, 11tr, 13br, 15br, 25, 31.

9 8 7 6 5 4 3 2 1

CONTENTS

TOP SECRET

Nearly every nation has a secret service that watches its enemies. The secret service **agents** do dangerous and exciting work and they often have to be ruthless and cunning.

Shhh... It's a Secret!

Secret services are... secret! It's hard to find out exactly what they do. Some of the work is so secret, that even the spies or agents don't have much information about it. Each agent usually knows only a few other agents, and they only know about their own mission. Then if they are caught—or if they **defect**—they can't give away too many secrets.

The headquarters of the British Secret Intelligence Service (SIS), also known as MI6, are in London.

Home and Away

Secret service agents can work in their own country or abroad. Sometimes the agents need to work in an enemy country to discover secrets. They try to uncover military plans, details of weapons, and where important places like weapon stores are. At home, they try to uncover **enemy agents**, track criminal gangs, or prevent crimes and terrorist attacks.

Disguised tools, such as this lipstick knife, can help secret service agents escape if they are captured.

Spy Talk

"Case Officers… plan and carry out **covert** intelligence operations overseas. Spending time in London, as well as abroad, they gather the secret **intelligence** the Government needs to promote and defend UK national interests. We are particularly interested in people with skills in Mandarin, Arabic, **Dari, Farsi, and Pashto**." *MI6 website, October 2008, encouraging people to apply to be spies.*

Top Secret

The Chinese secret service used a special Chinese language, spoken by very few people, to keep its messages safe from spies. The US army used the same trick in World War II, using the Native American Navajo language.

BEHIND ENEMY LINES

The most dangerous work that secret service agents have to carry out is in enemy territory. Here, spies are usually alone and often in great danger.

Nazis in Europe

In World War II, German **Nazi** forces invaded and **occupied** many countries in Europe. Most local people did not want the Nazis to be there, and some worked secretly against them.

The Special Operations Executive

The SOE was a secret service formed by British intelligence to fight Nazi Germany from behind enemy lines. It was dangerous work. **Undercover** SOE agents learned how to make explosions and kill with their bare hands. Then they moved to France to live a false life, with fake identity papers.

These rubber feet were used to make fake footprints in the sand of a French beach. The idea was to lead German soldiers in the wrong direction.

Sabotage and Subversion

The mission of the SOE was "**sabotage** and **subversion**." SOE agents blew up bridges, trains, and roads so that it was hard for the Nazis to move troops and weapons around. They helped local people to fight the Nazis. They also gathered information about enemy movements and plans, and passed these back to Britain in coded radio broadcasts.

Women Undercover

Of the 470 SOE agents in France, 39 were women. They were very brave and took great risks. Some were captured by the Nazis and killed. Odette Sansom was a successful and heroic secret agent in the SOE. She and her husband were betrayed by a **double agent** and caught by the Nazis. Odette was imprisoned in Ravensbrück **Concentration Camp** and tortured, but survived the ordeal.

Odette Sansom worked for the SOE from 1942 to 1945. After the war she was awarded the George Cross by the British and the Legion d'Honneur by the French.

Top Secret

During World War II, secret service agents dressed a dead body as an army officer and put fake plans for an invasion in his pocket. They dumped the body in the sea near Spain. The Germans found him, believed the plans were real, and moved their troops away from the area where the real invasion was to take place.

EAST vs. WEST

After World War II, the world was divided between the **communists** in the East and the **capitalists** in the West. Each side was suspicious of the other—the **Cold War** had begun.

A Climate of Fear

Both sides built up stocks of weapons, including nuclear bombs. Each had enough weapons to destroy the other. They also had secret services that kept spies busy checking what the other side was doing. They **tapped** phones, planted double agents, passed secret messages, and killed anyone who got in their way.

A nuclear test explosion was carried out by the United States in the 1950s. Both the United States and the USSR built enough nuclear weapons to destroy the world.

KGB

The KGB was the secret service of the **USSR**. It spied on **Eastern bloc** citizens to find any traitors or people opposed to communism. The KGB sent spies to Britain and the United States to steal information about weapons development and to try to get an early warning of any planned attack.

Following the Russian Revolution in 1917, Felix Dzershinsky (1877-1926) founded the all-powerful Bolshevik (communist) secret police, the Cheka. This organization made sure that opponents of the Bolsheviks and other "enemies of the state" were arrested and either imprisoned or executed without trial. The Cheka was a direct forerunner of the KGB.

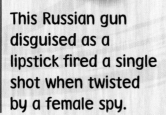

This Russian gun disguised as a lipstick fired a single shot when twisted by a female spy.

Top Secret

The KGB had a special trick called the "honey trap." A beautiful Russian spy would befriend foreign visitors to the USSR, particularly those suspected of spying. If the Western spy fell in love with the girl and told her secrets, she passed them to the KGB.

Eyes in the Skies

In the West, the CIA (Central Intelligence Agency) in the United States and MI5 in the United Kingdom tried to outwit the KGB. It was so difficult to get agents into the USSR that the U.S. developed advanced spy planes that could fly so high that they could not be shot down. The planes took photos of weapons, submarines, and airfields.

In the 1950s, the United States developed a lightweight spy plane, the U-2. However, in 1960 a Russian missile shot down a U-2 over Soviet territory, and the pilot, Gary Powers, was captured.

Information Wanted

Both the East and the West used informants —people who worked with secret information and passed it to enemy spies. Some were recruited when they already had their jobs, but others were trained spies who then applied for jobs that would bring secret information into their hands.

Some secret agents on both sides carried cyanide pills so that they could easily kill themselves if captured by the enemy.

Deadly Secrets

At the start of the Cold War, the U.S. had nuclear weapons, and the USSR wanted to catch up. Some KGB spies had high-level jobs in the U.S. helping to develop new nuclear weapons. Their mission was to pass on U.S. nuclear secrets to their KGB contacts. In 1951, Ethel and Julius Rosenberg were accused of giving the KGB information which made it possible for the USSR to build a nuclear bomb. The Rosenbergs were the first Americans to be executed for spying.

The Space Race

The race between the USSR and the U.S. to put humans into space, and on to the moon, took the Cold War into space. Both sides were afraid that the other would spy on them using satellites in space, or launch weapons from space, so each side tried to stay ahead of the other.

SPY FILE

TED HALL (1925-99)

Theodore "Ted" Hall was working in the U.S. to develop the atomic bomb. He passed information to the USSR that helped them to build a nuclear weapon many years earlier than they would otherwise have done. He was never punished for spying and eventually moved to Britain.

Spy satellites take photographs of areas that spies cannot visit.

SPYING ON EACH OTHER

Many secret services spy on their own people—especially in countries where the people are not happy with their lives but are not allowed to speak out or leave.

A Split City

Germany was divided into East and West parts from 1945 until 1990. For much of the Cold War, the city of Berlin was divided by a huge wall into East and West Berlin. With both sides so close to each other, Berlin was teeming with spies.

The Brandenburg Gate was on the West side of the city of Berlin. During the time when the Berlin Wall divided the city, the Gate was closed. On the Eastern side, rows of barricades and barbed wire were meant to discourage escape attempts.

ACHTUNG! Sie verlassen jetzt WEST-BERLIN

Everyone's a Spy

Many East German spies were spying on other East Germans. People in East Berlin had a hard life, and many wanted to escape to the West. The East German secret service, the Stasi, watched for people trying to escape. Ordinary people were encouraged to become informants, telling the Stasi about any suspicious behavior or anything **unpatriotic** they heard anyone say. Friends and neighbors spied on each other.

An East German officer examines a secret tunnel. It was built and used by East Berliners to escape to West Berlin.

Top Secret

When the Stasi interviewed anyone, they collected samples of the person's sweat on a cloth placed on their chair. The cloth was kept in a jar. If the Stasi later decided to arrest the person, they let a dog smell the cloth and then hunted the person down.

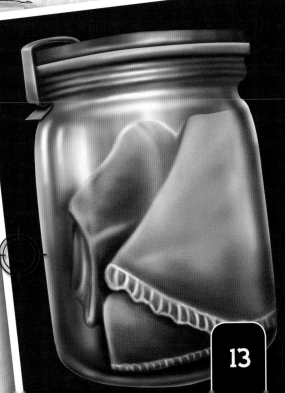

The Stasi kept shelves of "smell jars" with samples of the sweat of East Germans.

Collecting Evidence

The Stasi kept records on all East German citizens. These listed anything a person had said that might be against the state, and might even list what food they had eaten. The Stasi tapped telephone calls and used informers to gather information. After the Stasi was broken up in 1989, people were allowed to see their files. Many were horrified at how much detail they contained.

In the last days of the Stasi, workers in the Stasi headquarters began shredding the files and records. There are more than 16,000 bags of shredded documents.

Hunting Communists

It was not only the East that spied on their own people during the Cold War. In the United States, the government was very afraid that communists might take over. The CIA arrested, **interrogated**, and imprisoned many innocent people. The CIA often targeted writers they thought held "anti-American" views.

Writers and the KGB

Within the USSR, the KGB also kept a close watch on Russian citizens, especially anyone who grumbled about their lives. People who spoke out against communism, or who spoke in favor of religion, were called **dissidents**. They were often arrested, interrogated, and then sent to prisons or gulags—work camps. Writers were often the target of KGB investigations.

JURGEN G.

A man known as "Jurgen G." was arrested in Germany in 2003. He was accused of leading a secret Stasi death squad that killed East Germans who tried to escape to the West during the Cold War. But he had covered his tracks so successfully there was not enough evidence to find him guilty.

This phone tapping device could be hidden inside an old-style telephone.

SPYING ON CRIME

The secret services are often used to stop crimes. Agents might become members of drug-dealing and smuggling groups, or deal with crimes involving national security.

Fighting the Gangs

Large organized criminal gangs such as the **Mafia** (that began in Italy) and the **Triads** (from China and Hong Kong) work in many countries. They often bully businesses into paying **protection money**. If the owners refuse to pay, the gang kills them, or makes sure their business fails. The Mafia and Triads run illegal businesses of their own, making large amounts of money. They are often involved in smuggling drugs, weapons, and even illegal human **immigrants** or slaves.

This photograph shows the burnt-out wreckage of cars following a bomb attack on an anti-Mafia judge and his bodyguards in Palermo, Italy. The Mafia assassinated the judge with a remote-controlled car bomb during his investigation into **organized crime**.

Threatening Behavior?

U.S. Secret Service agents protect the president, accompanying him whenever he appears in public. They try to guard him against assassination attempts. The secret service investigates and checks people who will come into contact with the president and whom they suspect may be a threat.

Secret Service agents protect the U.S. president during a parade in Washington, D.C.

Top Secret

Playing the Game

Secret service agents often have to join a criminal gang. They pretend that they are criminals. They win the trust of the gang and act as a member. They pass information they learn to the secret services or the police. The information is used to stop criminal activities or to arrest gang leaders.

Listening In

Secret services use traditional methods, such as **phone taps** and hidden cameras, as well as newer technology, to help them capture criminals. They spy on text messages, listen in on cell phone conversations, and read the e-mails of a suspect. They can even find out what web pages someone's computer has displayed and where someone is from the signal of their cell phone.

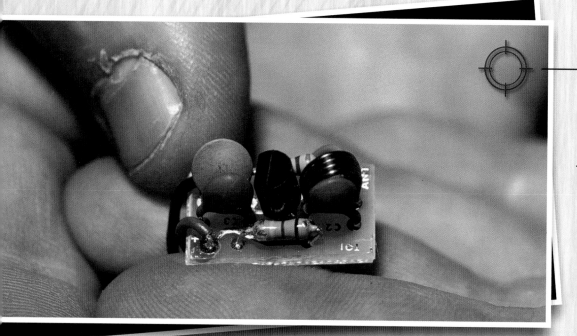

Some listening devices are now so tiny that they are little bigger than a fingernail.

SPY FILE

Secret service agents often spy illegally. From 1924 to 1972, FBI agents planted bugs and wire taps on people in the United States even though it wasn't allowed by law. They broke into buildings, stole evidence about the FBI's own activities, and covered up its mistakes. Some people even think that former President John F. Kennedy, who was shot in 1963, was killed by the CIA.

Electronic Ears

The secret services can use an electronic service called Echelon to listen in on any conversations. Echelon is said to scan all phone and Internet communications around the world looking for suspicious words. If it finds anything, the message is checked by a human investigator. If it still looks suspicious, the people sending and receiving the messages will be watched. Echelon is organized jointly by Australia, Canada, New Zealand, the United Kingdom, and the United States.

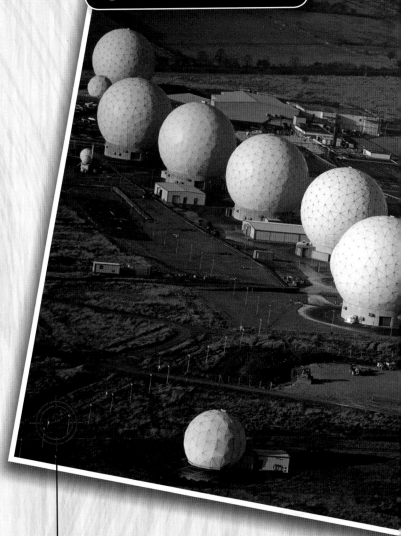

Equipment at Menwith Hill, United Kingdom, may be used by Echelon to monitor telecommunications.

Top Secret

Protecting China
The Chinese secret service has a "golden shield" program to monitor all phone calls, text messages, online chats, and e-mails of suspected criminals. This program can trace people in China who read or write on web sites and blogs that speak out against the Chinese system.

INSIDE ISRAEL

Mossad is the Israeli secret service that hunts down enemies of Israel. Its agents work around the world.

Escape to Safety

During World War II, **Nazi** Germany sent millions of Jewish people to die in concentration camps. An organization, Mossad, was set up to help Jews to escape from the Nazis to safety. Later, Mossad became the Israeli secret service. One of their goals was to hunt down the top Nazis who had ordered the deaths of the Jews.

Nazi-Hunting

In 1960, Mossad agents found Nazi war criminal Adolf Eichmann in Argentina. In a daring illegal raid, they kidnapped him and smuggled him to Israel, where he was tried and **executed**.

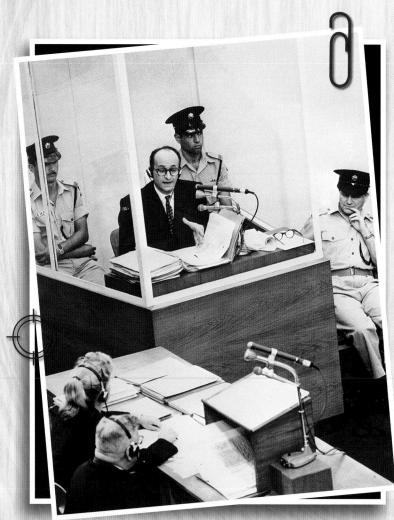

Surrounded by guards and standing in a bulletproof glass booth, former **SS** officer Adolf Eichmann testifies at his trial in Jerusalem in 1961.

Getting Weapons

While the U.S. and the USSR were spying on each other's nuclear weapons, Mossad agents set out to steal the information they needed to build nuclear weapons for Israel. They obtained the plans for a secret French jet, the Mirage 5, and then stole a ship full of **uranium**. When the ship was found, the uranium was missing. Using the French plans, Israel built its Nesher and Kfir jets, which are exact copies of the Mirage 5.

Israeli Kfir jets, based on stolen plans for the French Mirage 5

Modern Enemies

The state of Israel is on land that once belonged to Palestine. Mossad's biggest enemies today are Palestinians and other Arab groups which believe the land still belongs to Palestine. The pro-Palestinian group, Hamas, is Mossad's main target.

Death at the Games

Armed police drop into position on a terrace above the apartments where the members of the Israeli Olympic team were being held hostage.

Black September was a Palestinian terrorist group. They kidnapped and killed many Israeli athletes at the Olympic Games in Munich in 1972. For 20 years, Mossad ruthlessly hunted down the Black September terrorists. The mastermind behind the Black September attack is the only one still alive, but no one knows where he is.

Storming the Airport

In 1976, a plane flying from Israel to France was hijacked by anti-Israeli terrorists. It was landed at Entebbe airport in Uganda, where more than 100 passengers and crew were held hostage in the airport. Mossad built up a detailed picture of it from secret photographs and building plans. With Mossad's help, the Israeli army stormed the airport in the middle of the night, killing the hijackers and freeing the hostages.

The hijacked Air France jet stands abandoned at Entebbe airport in Uganda. Israeli commandos carried out a daring rescue mission and saved the lives of more than 100 hostages.

Top Secret

In 1997, two Mossad agents working in Jordan sprayed nerve poison into the ear of a Hamas leader in broad daylight. The man was soon vomiting and close to death. The agents were caught and beaten up by bodyguards, and Israel was quickly forced to supply the antidote to the poison so that the victim could be saved.

LICENSED TO KILL

Many secret services have assassination squads. Their targets are political leaders, master criminals, enemy spies, or enemies of the country.

Castro's Beard

For many years the United States thought that the communist country of Cuba would help the USSR to attack the United States. So the CIA launched "Operation Mongoose" in the 1960s to kill the leader of Cuba, Fidel Castro. They tried lots of very strange ways to kill him or make him look foolish in front of his people. They sent him a present of his favorite cigars, infected with a deadly disease, and planned to put salts into his boots to make his beard fall out. But all attempts failed!

Between 1960 and 1965, the CIA was involved in eight plots to assassinate Fidel Castro, the president of Cuba.

"It Wasn't Us"

Sometimes a secret service **frames** someone else for a killing. In 1981, there was an attempt to kill Pope John Paul II. The West blamed the Bulgarian secret service, and the Bulgarian government blamed the CIA or the Italian secret service, SISMI. The KGB and the Stasi have also been blamed, but no one really knows who was responsible.

Ways of Killing

The secret services are always developing better ways of killing their enemies. Bulgarian secret service agents killed Georgi Markov in London with a poison pellet fired from a specially adapted umbrella in 1978. In 2006, the Russian secret service was accused of killing ex-secret agent Alexander Litvinenko in London by putting **radioactive** poison in his food.

Trigger to fire the gun

Gas cylinder to make the umbrella work like a gun

Poison pellet fired from here

An umbrella was changed into a weapon to kill Georgi Markov.

SPY TALK

"It was considered in our service that poison is an easier weapon than a pistol." Alexander Litvinenko, former officer of the Russian state security service, murdered in 2006.

HUNT FOR TERRORISTS

Secret services spend a lot of time hunting down terrorists and trying to prevent terrorist attacks. The United States leads the world's "war on terrorism," but it is new to the fight. Other secret services have dealt with terrorism for much longer.

Tracking al-Qaeda

On September 11, 2001, al-Qaeda terrorists attacked the World Trade Center in New York City. Thousands of people were killed, and the buildings, called the Twin Towers, were destroyed. Since then the CIA has traced many al-Qaeda groups and training camps in places such as the Middle East, Pakistan, and Afghanistan. As well as spies, the CIA uses spy technology to intercept messages and spy satellites to find camps and stores of weapons.

The Twin Towers of the World Trade Center in New York, before the attack in September 2001

Cells and Schools

Al-Qaeda terrorists work in small groups called cells. Each person has a normal life with a job and a family as their cover. But secretly they are part of a group planning terrorist attacks around the world. Many terrorists are trained at special camps, some in Pakistan and Afghanistan. Secret services trying to prevent terrorism look out for people who visit those countries without their families, and who have contact with other known terrorist suspects.

Recruits at an al-Qaeda training camp. At these camps they receive instruction on fitness and how to use different weapons.

Getting it Wrong

When the British secret service, MI5, tried to recruit more Asian Muslim agents to help them track down Islamic terrorist groups, they recruited some people who were already working for al-Qaeda. The al-Qaeda agents offered their services—they worked undercover for the British intelligence and told al-Qaeda how MI5 was working against them.

Fighting Dirty

Secret services sometimes use illegal methods themselves to get information from people they capture. MI5, the British army and police, and the U.S. secret services have been accused of torturing suspects for information about terrorist activities. The **Chechen government** says the Russian secret service has carried out terrorist attacks in Russia and blamed Chechen terrorists for them.

Terrorist Tigers

Some secret services help terrorist groups in other countries. The Tamil Tigers are a terrorist group who want a separate country for the Tamil people in Sri Lanka, an island near India. Many Tamil terrorists have been trained in Israel by Mossad.

These female fighters from the Tamil Tigers are at their base, northeast of Colombo, Sri Lanka. The Tamil Tigers developed as a fearsome fighting force in the early 1970s, attacking Sri Lankan armed forces and political targets.

Olympic Spies

China is a secretive country with a long history of spying. When it hosted the Olympic Games in 2008, the director of security, Qiang Wei, had a budget of $1.3 billion to protect the Games from terrorist attacks and to uncover any foreign secret agents disguised as sports staff or journalists. Many official visitors from Western countries were warned that hotel staff would search their rooms and check electronic devices for useful contact details. They were told to take pay-as-you-go cell phones and throw them away after the trip.

SPY TALK

"Terrorists are often... made up simply of family members. It's very hard to penetrate such groups. A cell made up of two brothers and a cousin, how can you penetrate that cell?... During the Cold War... we knew who the other side's spies or intelligence officers were, and we could gain access to them. That's a big difference between the Cold War and today."
Larry Kolb,
ex-Cold War spy

Chinese security officers with with sniffer dogs patrol the "bird's nest" stadium in Beijing before the opening of the Olympic Games in 2008.

GLOSSARY

assassination squad   group of people trained to kill

capitalist   person who owns property and businesses that are run for profits

Chechen government   the government of the Chechen Republic, a region which claims independence from Russia. The government is not recognized by other countries.

Cold War   period from the 1950s to 1990 when countries in the East and the West were enemies and on the brink of war

communist   person who believes that all property and businesses should be owned by the government

concentration camp   harsh prison where many people are kept in terrible conditions

covert   secret

Dari, Farsi, and Pashto languages spoken in the Middle East. Dari and Pashto are spoken in Afghanistan, and Farsi is the official language of Iran.

defect   when a spy leaves his own country to spy for another country

dissident   someone who speaks out against the political system of their own country

double agent   someone who pretends to be working for one organization, but is actually working for the opposition

Eastern bloc   group of Communist countries in Eastern Europe in the second half of the twentieth century

enemy agent   spy working for the other side in a conflict

execute   kill a person, usually when it has been decided by a party or system of government

frame   make it look as if someone is guilty of a crime when they are not

immigrant person moving into a country from abroad

intelligence information gathering activites

interrogate question severely and closely

Mafia brutal gang of criminals and gangsters that started in Italy but now has members worldwide

national security protecting the state from attack, either by terrorists or enemy powers

Nazi member of a political party that seized control in Germany under Adolf Hitler in 1933

occupied controlled by a foreign army

organized crime crime which is planned and carried out on a large scale by a structured group

phone tap equipment to listen in on or record telephone conversations secretly

protection money bribe paid to a gangster or criminal gang to avoid violence

radioactive producing energy from the breakdown of atoms (very small particles of matter)

sabotage destroy something deliberately

SS military force within the Nazi party in Germany during WWII. The SS provided Adolf Hitler's bodyguard and also concentration camp guards

subversion work to undermine or bring down a system

Triads secret criminal groups that started in China

undercover working secretively

unpatriotic not showing any love for one's country or care for its defense

uranium a metallic element which can be used to produce nuclear weapons

USSR Union of Soviet Socialist Republics—a former communist country which used to consist of Russia and 14 other states. It broke up in 1991.

INDEX

WEB FINDER

www.cia.gov/about-cia/cia-museum/cia-museum-tour/index.html
Interactive tour of an online museum of spy tools and objects

http://edition.cnn.com/specials/cold.war/
All about the Cold War and the spies that made it possible

www.bbc.co.uk/history/worldwars/wwtwo/soe_01.shtml
All about how the SOE was formed and worked